I AM
Creating My
Own Happiness

by
Barry Thomas Bechta

**UNCONDITIONAL
LOVE BOOKS**

*Redefining, Guiding, and Inspiring Humanity's
Connection to the Creative Power within.*

I AM Creating My Own Happiness
by
Barry Thomas Bechta

© 2009 by BARRY THOMAS BECHTA

Library and Archives Canada Cataloguing in Publication

Bechta, Barry Thomas, 1968-
   I am creating my own happiness / by Barry Thomas Bechta.

ISBN 978-0-9686835-6-9

   1. Happiness--Religious aspects.
2. Self-realization--Religious aspects. I. Title.

BL65.H36B42 2009   204   C2009-905995-9

I AM
Creating My
Own Happiness

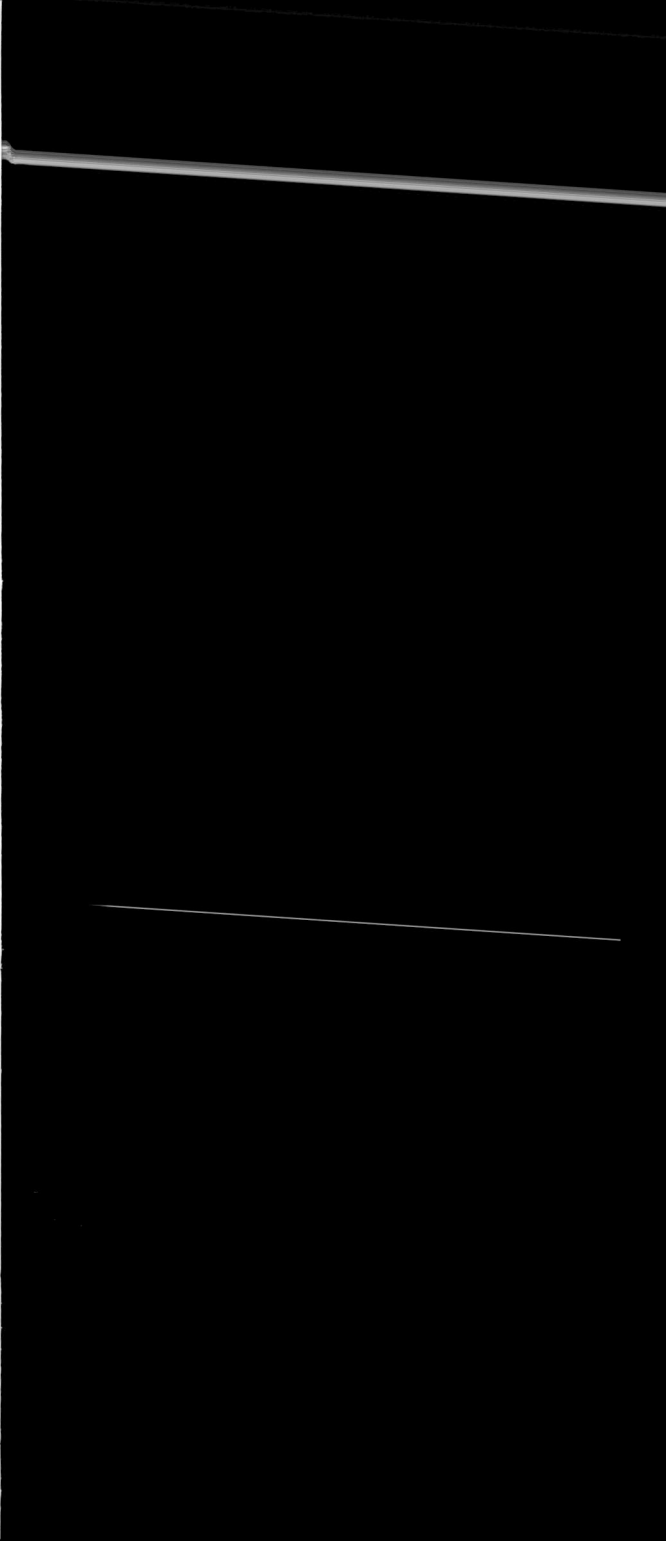

What is the Happiest thought I can imagine in this situation right Here right Now?

When I Joyfully
express what is in my heart and
at the same time Serve God in others,
then I AM One with God's Purpose
for my life.   When I feel I have to force
one or the other then I am separate
from that Connection and separate
from the Source and Supply
of my Happiness.

ACKNOWLEDGEMENTS

GOD

Ellen and Clare

Binah, Anthony, and Zac

Stephen, Margaret, Gabe, and Sam

Melinda, Paul, Sydney, and Gryphon

Everyone whom has ever been a part of my life

Everyone whom has ever helped me to be more in my life

I Thank God for each and everyone of your loving hearts.

And most importantly,

I THANK YOU

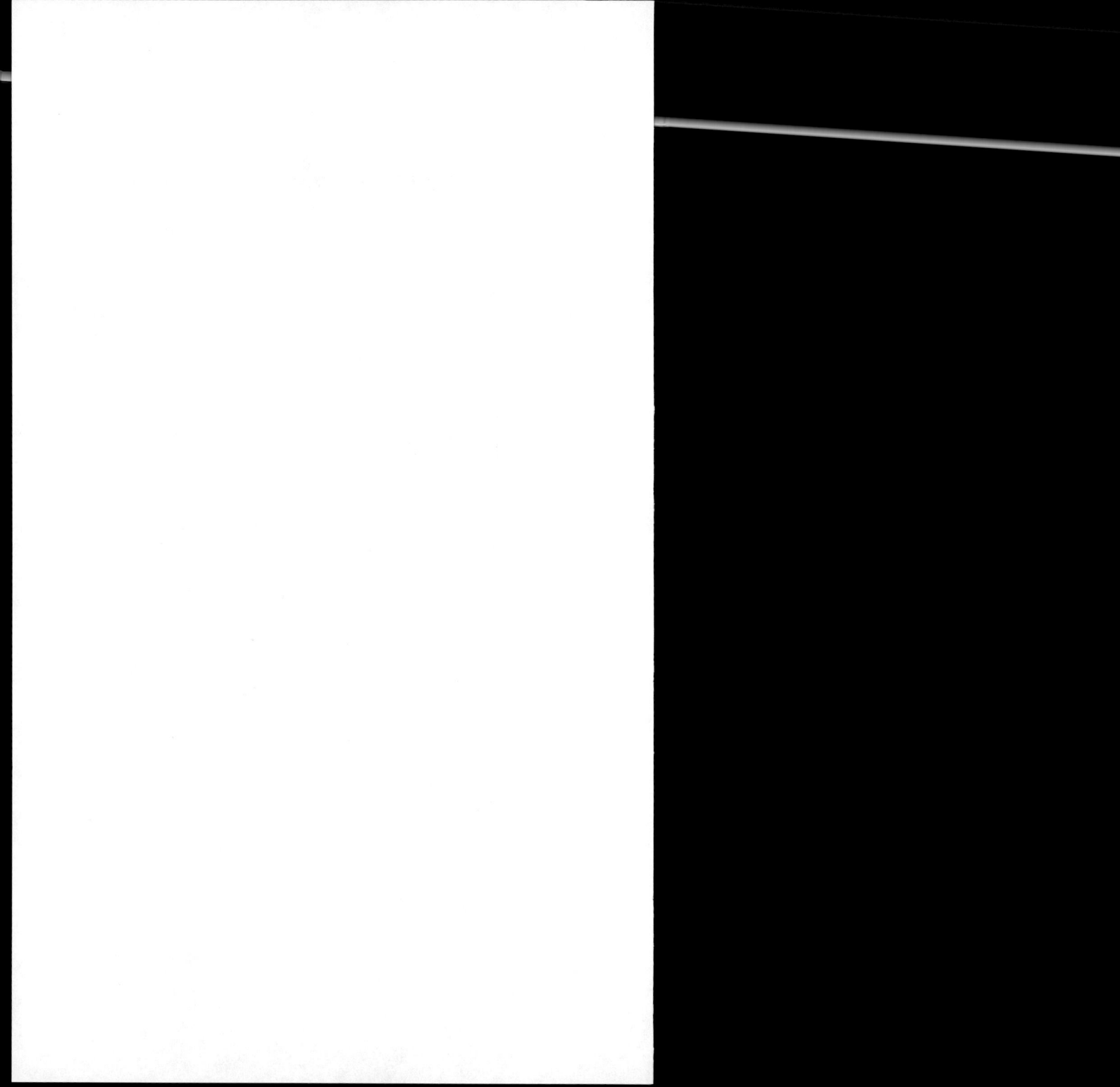

TO THE READER

What is the Happiest thought you can imagine right Now? What would bring you the most Joy Now Here and serve God in others at the same time? What would Love Joyfully do Now Here? Therein lies the answers to your Lasting Happiness.

No person, place, thing, or experience in the outer world can make you feel Happy. You Choose it. Unless and until you develop your Connection to God within, you go without. When you accept your unity with God and draw everything from God's Presence within you, then and only then can you Consciously Be in a state of Lasting Happiness.

Love, Joy, Success, Abundance, and Happiness are some of the names applied to God's Natural Life Giving State of Being. You are these attributes when you Choose to Be. Always in all ways it is your Choice.

Your mind holds your Intentions for your life experience. Your mind can only hold one thought at a time. You Choose whether your One thought is of fear and limitations, or of God and Good. Your thoughts and the life they Create for you are your Responsibility to Choose. Yours and yours alone.

You can and do Choose for others to join in your life. First and foremost you Choose God to Guide and Provide for you. Next, you Choose the people, places, things, and experiences that support your dreams. Finally, you Choose to live the life you desire. No one else can take that Responsibility. Many people join in your life Creation and Dreams, as you do in theirs, however You are Responsible for Creating only your own experience.

Your thoughts, feelings, words, and actions Choose whether your experiences are ungodly or Godly. In every moment, you Choose to Be God awful or God Awe Full.

God, Love, and Life are synonymous. God uses every part of All That Is to Communicate with you. Every part of life Encourages you to Unify with God. Within you is your direct Connection to God and your Dreams and your Lasting Happiness. When you Choose God, God Supports and Supplies All That Is in your life, but God waits until you Choose. Free Will is your ability to Choose to experience whatever you Choose.

There is no good or bad, there is only experience. God only

provides what you Choose through your Intention and Attention in your experience. The Law of Attraction means that Whatever you give your attention to, you Intend to include in your experience. Your thoughts about All That Is Asks the Universe to mirror your thoughts and provide more of the same experiences for you. When your Attention and intentions only see Happiness, that is what you experience. When you feel Joyful, that is what you are Creating.

Choose God's Lasting Happiness Always in All That Is
Barry Thomas Bechta

TABLE OF CONTENTS

I AM God's Happiness

God is All
God is All within me
I AM One within God
God, Love, and Life are the same
All communicate to me by my name
There is really Only One type of experience
I Access it through my personal preferences
Good or bad by my Beliefs and Attention
My Attention informs my Intentions
To give me more of my Beliefs
Of Good or grief

I AM God's Happiness

God is All
God is All within me
I AM One within God

God is All That Is. I AM a part of God. God is All within me. I AM One within God. God is Happiness. God is Wholeness. God is Complete. As a part of God, I AM too.

Everything that God Is, I AM. Everything that God Is, Everything Is. Everything is God. Only one thing can allow me to be separate from God. That one thing is my Thoughts.

My Thoughts inform my perceptions of my life. My Thoughts inform my Intentions for my life. My Thoughts can believe in separation from God, or accept my Unity with God. Only I Choose my Thoughts.

God is All Names and All Forms in my life experience, and God takes on many names and many forms by my Thoughts and my Thoughts alone. God is whatever I imagine, think, and believe God to be. Whatever I decide is manifest through my beliefs. Whatever I believe, I receive.

God gives me Free Will to choose whatever I desire to experience. Whatever I AM in my experience is what I have Chosen. Free Will is really Freedom of Choice to work without God, or work with God. It is my Choice. No matter what I Choose to call God (Universe, Mother Nature, Allah, Great Mystery, Chance, Higher Self, Soul, etcetera) God always provides what I decide about my life.

God, Love, and Life are the same
All communicate to me by my name

God, Love, and Life are different words describing the

same Energy. This God/Life/Energy manifests my energy use. My energy use can be ego energy or God Energy.

My energy has my name on it. My entire life experience speaks to me by name. God/Life/Energy can only speak to me by my Chosen name.

When I Choose to place my attention on the forms of experience, my lower vibration speaks my Chosen name, and God matches my Free Will Intentions.

When I Choose to place my attention on the feelings of experience, my Higher Vibration speaks my Chosen name, and God matches my Free Will Intentions.

Focussing on the forms of experience is lower vibrational. Ego energy is lower vibrational. Fear is lower vibrational. Hate is lower vibrational. Believing in lack and limitation is lower vibrational. Lower vibrational energy is dense and slow and associated with physicality. Lower vibrational energy pulls me down and disconnects me from God's Joy and Potential in my life.

God Energy is Higher Vibrational. The Feeling of God is Higher Vibrational. Faith is Higher Vibrational. Love is Higher Vibrational. Believing in Abundance and Potential is Higher Vibrational. Higher Vibrational Energy is ephemeral and fast and associated with spirituality. Higher Vibrational Energy Uplifts and Connects me with God's Joy and Potential in my life.

There is really Only One type of experience
I Assess it through my personal preferences

The Energy of God is the Only experience going. This experience is a Spiritual experience. The physicality of Life is actually composed primarily of empty space. That space is The Pure Potential of Spirit animating matter. All matter is Spirit animated. To experience more of God's Happiness in my life, I need only to focus on the Spirit within all matter.

There is Only One type of experience. This Spiritual experience of matter comes to me matching my energy use; low vibrational energy or High Vibrational Energy. Spirit Animates All

Matter. I Choose through my Attention, God Animates my Intentions.

God Animates my Choices and then I assess what I have in my life by my personal preferences, by my expectations, by my judgements. Either I AM Experiencing my desires or I am expecting them.

When I am expecting my desires, I am lower vibrational because I imagine I am without my desires. As a result I attract my lower vibrational experiences.

When I AM Experiencing my desires, I AM Higher Vibrational and One with God. I AM in the flow. I enjoy God and Love and Life and experience that I AM One within God. As a result I attract my Higher Vibrational experiences.

Good or bad by my Beliefs and Attention
My Attention informs my Intentions

There is only one type of experience (a Vibrational Energy Experience), yet there are infinite possibilities as to what that experience becomes through me. The quicker I Choose to see the Spirit within my experiences, the quicker I Choose to be one with the Higher Vibrational Energy of God.

To give me more of my Beliefs
Of Good or grief

Through my Beliefs and Attention, I Choose what type of energy I desire to call by my name. My Attention informs my Intentions. My Intentions inform my Choices. My Choices Attract my Experiences.

All experiences are in-formed by God's Spirit. God's Spirit is Happiness, Love, Success, Abundance, and High Vibrational Energy. When I accept that God's Happiness Creates all forms then I AM One with God.

My inner world of feelings Creates my outer world of forms. When I Choose God's Happiness as the Feeling within me, then my inner world manifests forms that match my inner feelings. Higher Vibrational Feelings Attract Higher Vibrational forms. All forms are Higher Vibrational when they are in-formed by God's Higher Vibrational Happiness. I know I AM Higher Vibrational when I feel Joyful, Confident, Successful, Abundant, and One with the flow of life. Joy is my Compass.

I AM GOD'S HAPPINESS

*When I Choose God's Happiness
as the Feeling within me, then my inner world
manifests forms that match my inner feelings.*

I AM Physical Happiness

Physical Happiness means Radiant Health
Physical Happiness means Abundant Wealth
God provides my Radiant Health and Beauty
God Provides everything through our shared Unity
God Provides me with individual talents and gifts
God Provides and Asks only that I share my gifts
When I share my talents with Love and Joy
God shares Happily through numerous toys
God gives Joyfully to me, I give Joyfully to God
Only in Physical form can I Express and
Create the forms that Bless God

I AM Physical Happiness

I AM PHYSICAL HAPPINESS

God is everything. God provides everything. There is only God. God Provides All That Is. God Provides All Physical Life. God Provides my physical form and experience. God Provides this endlessly, happily. God Provides Free Will. God allows each and every individualization of God the Free Will to Choose whatever, because in reality whatever, is God.

Whatever I Choose is God. Everything I experience is God's Energy. However my Choice can be to imagine I am separate from God's Energy or to unify with God. God's Free Will allows me to Freely Choose Whatever I Believe.

God has no preference in the matters of my life. God Loves me and Allows me to be, do, or have whatever I Choose. It is always my Choice. No matter how qualified or deserving I AM as an individualization of God, I only experience a more fulfilling life of Love, Success, Happiness, and Abundance when I can imagine it for myself and claim it with all of my thoughts, feelings, words, and actions using my whole heart, mind, and being. What I imagine, believe, accept, allow, and most importantly Choose is what I find, live, discover, experience. Physical Happiness is a Choice I can Choose or deny in my life experience.

Physical Happiness means Radiant Health
Physical Happiness means Abundant Wealth

I know what I AM Choosing by looking at the people, places, things, and experiences in my life. Absolutely everything in my life is there by MY Choice. Only I can Choose my life. Even when I imagine I give someone else the ability to Choose on my behalf, I have Chosen to allow whatever may come to me be my Choice (unconsciously). If I find I AM unhappy with my life, I have only to make a different Choice.

God provides my Radiant Health and Beauty
God Provides everything through our shared Unity

There is One very effective way to make a different Choice in my life and Create different and more desirable results. That One Choice is to make my Choices from a place of Power.

Power is only found in the Present moment through Unity with God. When I first Choose to see my Oneness with God and then make a decision, I can access All the Love, Success, Happiness, and Abundance available as God through me Right Here Right Now.

Analysing what happened in my past, or worrying about how my future will happen only takes me out of the Peace, Joy, Potential, and Power available Right Now. God is Now Here. Where do I Choose to Be?

When I Choose to be One with God, I Choose to Be One with my desired experience. I may not see it yet, but I can feel it. I feel Confident and Secure and Cared for when I Choose to Unify with God first and always.

When I Unify with God, I Choose to Be Peace, Joy, Patience, Love, Success, Happiness, Abundance; I Choose to Be anything and everything that is Life Affirming; God Affirming. Whatever I Choose, I AM. Whatever I AM, I experience. Either I am expecting my desires to happen or I AM Experiencing my desires Right Now.

I experience my desires much quicker when I Choose to Unify with God. God is Life. All of Life is God. If I fight against anything in my life, I fight God in my life; deny God in my life. When I discover that my life does not feel Good or Joyful in the moment, I Choose any thought that Aligns with Joy and Potential in my life. I know I have reconnected when I feel better, or Joyful, or a sense of relief.

God Provides me with individual talents and gifts
God Provides and Asks only that I share my gifts

One powerful way to align with God in my life is to use my individual talents and gifts for the benefit of others. God Provides me with individual talents and gifts for the benefit of the entire world. My talents and gifts are different from those of other people. Each and everyone of us holds individual talents and gifts for the benefit of the entire world.

When I use my talents and gifts for the benefit of the entire world, others are inspired to do the same. What I give, I live. It all starts with me. I AM the only one with the power to Create my experience. The only thing that can stop me from Creating my experience is myself. The way I create my experience, especially when I am on my own, affects the entire world experience.

When I share my talents with Love and Joy
God shares Happily through numerous toys

When I Choose Happiness as my Intention, I share my talents and gifts with Love and Joy. When I AM One with God, I AM All That Is. I AM Free, I do whatever brings Joy to myself and others, and I Have all I need. I have all I need because God shares Happily through numerous people, places, things, and experiences in my life.

God's gift to me is my life and my talents and my gifts. Everything I do with my life and my talents and my gifts is my gift back to God. Life is a circle of giving and receiving and giving and receiving.

Whatever I desire to experience, I give. God gives that same experience back to me multiplied immensely. God has the entire Universe to give through. All God Asks me is to share a portion of what I AM given.

Whatever I desire to experience more of I have but to know

that I AM That and share it with others. I can only receive what I am prepared to give. I Give Love, I Live Love. I Give Success, I Live Success. I Give Abundance, I Live Abundance. My thoughts, feelings, words, and actions Give my Creation Vibration its form.

God gives Joyfully to me, I give Joyfully to God Only in Physical form can I Express and Create the forms that Bless God

Only living as a human being on Earth am I able to experience separation from God. Only in physical form can I express and create forms that Bless, Honour, and Give to God. When I pass from this physical form and live in spirit, I AM One with God. There is no separation.

The Greatest Gift God has given me is Free Will and the ability to use it to Choose to Be Whole with God. God gives Joyfully to me the ability to Choose whatever I wish. When I recognize this and know that I Can Choose Unity over separation, I Joyfully give my thoughts and feelings to God.

I AM PHYSICAL HAPPINESS

The Greatest Gift God has given me is Free Will and the ability to use it to Choose to Be Whole with God.

I AM Mental Happiness

God Provides me with Free Will
Free Choice, Freedom, Free Will
I can Choose absolutely anything I desire
I can Choose Happiness or I can Choose hellfire
I Choose God as my Source and Supply
I Choose God as my ability to Fly
I Choose God within my darkest days
I Choose God through my thinking ways
I Choose God as my Joy and Happiness
I Choose God as my Tranquillity,
Peace, and my Eternal Bliss

I AM Mental Happiness

I AM MENTAL HAPPINESS

Peace of mind comes by my Choosing Happiness and Peace of mind in whatever is Happening. My access point to Happiness is found within whatever experience is Now Here. Every experience, no matter what appears to be, holds within it the potential for Peace and Happiness.

God Provides me with Free Will
Free Choice, Freedom, Free Will

Happiness occurs when I Freely Choose Happiness. No one can make me Choose Happiness. No one can make me Choose Sadness. God Provides me with the Free Will to Choose everything and anything I desire. I AM Free to Choose whatever I imagine. Everything presently in my life is there because I Chose it. My thoughts are Choosing Right Here Right Now.

I can Choose absolutely anything I desire
I can Choose Happiness or I can Choose hellfire

God Provides Love, Success, Abundance, and Happiness to me and every person, place, and thing in existence continually without fail. That is God's nature. God Gives Opulence Directly to All That Is.

God is All That Is. I imagine God as the Sun. I AM a candle within the body of the Sun. As a part of the Sun, my light is One with the Sun's Light. There is no way to identify my light apart from God's Light. God's Opulence cannot be experienced when directly in contact with God.

In order to experience God's Opulence, God forms the human experience. Through the human experience, God supports Free Will. Free Will is a mental construct separating my individuality from All That Is in order to experience All That Is.

From God's Perspective, there is Only Unity. From the human perspective, there is separation and Unity.

Through the human perspective, I live in a particular home in a particular city in a particular country on the planet Earth. I have particular friends. I work in a particular livelihood. I come from a particular family.

From God's Perspective I AM. I AM Every person, place, and thing. I live everywhere, every time, and everyone is me.

From the human perspective I am the only one. When I believe I am the only one, I will do absolutely anything to keep what I believe is mine.

From God's Perspective We Are All One. When We Are All One, I will give absolutely anything to support our Oneness.

When I try to control the flow of life, life can be a challenging struggle. When I go with the flow of life, life is easy and relaxed. The flow of life Creates Heaven on Earth.

Hell is my inability to control the flow of whatever is Now Here.

Heaven is my ability to allow the flow of whatever is Now Here.

I Choose God as my Source and Supply
I Choose God as my ability to Fly

It is my Choice alone to Choose God in every experience. Choosing God in every experience is Happy and Peaceful when I believe that is the case. The only thing I can control in life is my own thoughts, feelings, words, and actions.

Challenges are a way of life taught from birth through to death in the human experience. Even though I can only control my individual experience, the human experience teaches me, tells me, and shows me through example after example that people can control other people through all forms of thoughts, feelings, words, and actions. This belief system has been at the heart of the human experience for many eons. This system of beliefs champions a competition model of experience over a Cooperation model.

The competition model directs my world experience with life-destroying choices. Competition with other people, places, and things leads to the destruction of other people, places, and things. From the human competition perspective I am the only one. When I believe I am the only one, I will do absolutely anything to keep what I believe is mine.

The Cooperation model directs my world experience with Life-Affirming choices. Cooperation with other people, places, and things leads to the benefit of all people, places, and things. From God's Cooperation Perspective, We Are All One. When We Are All One, I will give absolutely anything to support our shared Oneness.

I Choose God within my darkest days
I Choose God through my thinking ways

When I accept that I have Chosen everything that makes my world experience what it is today, I allow the flow of whatever is. There is nothing I can do to change whatever is Now Here. Whatever is Now Here in my experience Is only present for me to Love and Accept it.

When I fight to control whatever is Now Here. All the power I use to fight it I also us to energize it. Whatever I give my attention to, I include in my experience. The Universe matches my energy use and gives me more of whatever I energize.

When I allow the flow of whatever is Now Here and I love and accept it fully, I AM Happy. Happiness allows What Is in the present moment and imagines what can be different in the next moment.

My darkest days are attracted by my thoughts and feelings about them. I Choose hell through thoughts and feelings that deny my Joy and Potential.

I Choose Heaven through thoughts and feelings that support my Joy and Potential.

I Choose God as my Joy and Happiness
I Choose God as my Tranquillity,
Peace, and my Eternal Bliss

God is All That Is. In the human experience God is a Choice. To experience God, I Choose God. There is no other way. Choosing God is Choosing Love, Success, Abundance, Happiness, Faith, and Fulfilment.

To Choose Mental Happiness in everything, I Consciously Choose thoughts that Connect me with God's Joy and Potential in my life.

I AM MENTAL HAPPINESS

To Choose Mental Happiness in everything,
I Consciously Choose thoughts that Connect me with
God's Joy and Potential in my life.

I AM Emotional Happiness

My Emotions push for results over imagination
My ego (emotionally guided opinions) chooses separation
My ego believes in separation from God and all others
My ego believes it Must be, do, and have over others
God Manifests whatever in my life I Choose to begin
My ability to Manifest matches my ability to Imagine
My inability to Manifest begins and ends with me
My ability to Manifest my Oneness is within me
I Choose to Imagine what I would like to experience
Being One with these results in Spirit form
Manifests them in Opulence

I AM Emotional Happiness

I AM EMOTIONAL HAPPINESS

My emotionally guided opinions (ego) Must be, do, or have particular experiences. My ego believes I am separate from God and others. My ego struggles to change, Create, get, and improve my outer experiences. My ego looks to past and future Happiness. My ego works hard and uses my will power to achieve results.

God (Giving Ongoing Directly) within me Can be, do, or have any experience. I AM One with God and all others. God reminds me to Allow, Accept, Connect with, and Be Aware of my Oneness with any experience I can imagine. God reminds me that Happiness is only found in the present moment and experience Now Here. God easily and effortlessly Manifests as my reality whatever I believe is my reality or I Imagine is possible.

My Emotions push for results over imagination
My ego (emotionally guided opinions) chooses separation

My ego thrives on guilt and blame. My ego fights for everything in my life accepts separation as reality. There is nothing that Is separate unless my thinking makes it so. It is a Choice. Choosing guilt and blame fosters a downward spiral filled with more guilt and blame. Guilt and blame are easy to believe when I accept the ego point of view that imagines everything is separate from everything else. My ego uses my imagination.

My ego uses emotions. Emotions are very persuasive tools in life. Emotions push for immediate results over the time and energy involved in imagining best case scenarios. My imagination can also be used to Create whatever I focus upon.

God is the best case scenario. It is my responsibility to Choose God as the best case scenario in every moment Now Here. I can only take Responsibility for the things I Create. Taking Responsibility means that I Accept that I Create absolutely everything in my experience.

The ego based life is full of guilty pressure.

The God based life is full of Responsible Pleasure.

My ego believes in separation from God and all others
My ego believes it Must be, do, and have over others

Emotions at their worst are angry, anxious, and desperate. Emotions at their best are Loving and Compassionate.

When my ego (emotionally guided opinions) is at the centre of any of my thoughts, feelings, words, and actions, it calls angrily, anxiously, and desperately for love. This call for love is disguised within the pursuit to be, do, or have particular people, places, things, and experiences in my life. My ego believes I win with these things or lose without them. My ego believes it is separate from all these things, from All That Is, and ultimately from God. My ego angrily, anxiously, and desperately fights to secure the things I so angrily, anxiously, and desperately desire.

God Manifests whatever in my life I Choose to begin
My ability to Manifest matches my ability to Imagine

God Is All. There is nothing that God Is Not. God is the fulfilment of All That Was, Is, and Will Be. God is the Energy of All Life. God provides Free Will and Allows me to experience whatever I Choose, whatever I desire, and whatever I can Imagine.

In my past, I Chose to Align with, Allow, and Accept my emotionally guided opinions in my life experience. My ego used all of it's tools to emotionally wrap me up with it's agenda. My ego pulled convincingly at my Heart and Mind to fulfil ego's desires.

In the largest scale, my ego is my emotionally guided opinions. I Choose all my opinions including my emotionally guided ones. God Allows me to experience my Choices. My Choices have come to me powerfully. Many times my ability to manifest matched my ability to imagine my emotionally guided opinions as my reality.

I AM Grateful for my emotionally guided opinions. My emotionally guided opinions are a part of me. To deny my ego, is a Choice to rely on my ego. Whatever I deny, fight, condemn, judge, and oppose is also what I Choose to Align with, Allow, and Accept in my life as my deepest heartfelt most secret beliefs.

My inability to manifest begins and ends with me
My ability to Manifest my Oneness is within me

Whatever I Choose to Align with, Allow, and Accept in my life is what I Choose to Manifest. I always in all ways manifest whatever I Align with, Allow, and Accept as my life through my thoughts and feelings.

In my past, I felt frustrated with my inability to manifest my dreams. The deeper reality was that in fact I was using my ability perfectly, to manifest the lack of my dreams I focussed on. I ignored the fact that I Choose to Align with, Allow, and Accept my disappointments over my dreams.

In all of my Life, my ability to manifest has never been a problem. My challenge has been only to Consciously Choose absolutely everything that I Intended to Manifest.

I Forgive myself in the forms of every person, place, thing, and experience that came into my life so that I could live my beliefs and then Chose to Align with, Allow, and Accept a fuller Conscious experience.

I Love every person, place, thing, and experience in my life that has lead me to be Who and What I AM today. I Love everything about my past. I Love everything in my world experience Right Here Right Now because all of it makes me Who I AM Today. However my history only becomes my destiny if I Choose to believe that is so. My dreams become my reality when I believe they are so.

I Intend to Align with, Allow, and Accept my dreams as my life. I Intend to Align with, Allow, and Accept God's Vision of my dreams as my life. God's Vision of my dreams and life is the most Loving, Peaceful, Joyous, Abundant, Successful, and

Miraculous Experience that I Can Choose to Align with, Allow and Accept as my life.

I Choose to Imagine what I would like to experience Being One with these results in Spirit form Manifests them in Opulence

I Can Choose whatever I imagine to become my life experience. Anything I Can Align with, Allow, and Accept as Being Here Now, God Can Manifest Instantaneously. God Can Do Anything.

I AM EMOTIONAL HAPPINESS

I Can Choose whatever I imagine to become my life experience. Anything I Can Align with, Allow, and Accept as Being Here Now, God Can Manifest Instantaneously.

I AM Spiritual Happiness

All the Love of my life is Now within me
This Love is God's Powerful Divine Qualities
Love pursued in the outside world disappears
Love uncovered inside of me attracts no fears
I Love myself and my life fully inside and out
I Choose Love, Success, and Abundance over doubt
Being disconnected or Connected to God is a Choice
I Claim my Connection with God through my voice
I Breathe in Deeply and use God's name (AH)
I exhale deeply (OM) and transform my tension
back into the energy of God

I AM Spiritual Happiness

I AM SPIRITUAL HAPPINESS

When I AM in the Now, when I AM in the Present Moment, there is no time. Being in the flow is timeless. When life becomes timeless, I AM One with God. One with All Potential. When I AM One with God my life flows easily. When my life flows easily, I AM Happy.

All the Love of my life is Now within me
This Love is God's Powerful Divine Qualities

Perception is a function of the mind. Something may seem to occur outside of me, yet the only place I experience anything is within me. All of my life is experienced within me. Every person, place, and thing, I experience, I experience within me.

The Feeling of Love is something I feel within me. All the Love I will ever experience in my life is presently residing within me. The Love I experience in life from family, friends, and intimate partners comes from within me and is presently residing within me.

Right Here Right Now I can access the Love I imagine comes from others even without them being here. I can also access the Love I imagine comes from others even when they seem to be angry with me. All the Love I feel in my life is accessed by my Choice to Connect with it. All of the Love I feel is within me.

Love pursued in the outside world disappears
Love uncovered inside of me attracts no fears

God Provides absolutely everything in life. I Choose through my Free Will what I Align with, Allow, and Accept into my life.

I rarely get the things I desire in life when I pursue them. The reason I rarely get them is that within my being I believe that I am separate from that particular thing when I *pursue* it and as a result this becomes my very experience – pursuit.

I always get the things I desire when I attract them into my life. The only way to Attract something into my life is by changing my inner belief of being separate from something to being One with something.

When I come from a place of being Whole and Complete just as I AM Right Here Right Now, then my Completeness Attracts my experience of all I desire. Being Complete means I already feel within my heart that I have something, even when it may not be present in my experience.

I experience my whole life from my perception inside of me. My mind can accept my perceived reality of What Is or my imagined reality of what I desire to be as both being real. There is no difference in my inner reality. God's Free Will Allows both realities to have whatever power I imbue them with. Whatever I can believe I can achieve.

Absolutely any belief I can Align with, Allow, and Accept within me, God can manifest instantly. God Can Do Anything.

God is waiting for me to Align with, Allow, and Accept everything in my life I believe is separate from me. Separation is just a belief. God Allows me to Choose whatever I decide through Free Will. I shall see in my physical experience whatever I desire to be as mine when I believe that whatever I desire is mine.

I Love myself and my life fully inside and out
I Choose Love, Success, and Abundance over doubt

I Love myself fully. I Love others fully. I Love God Fully. God is All of Life; every person, place, thing, and experience. The way to greater Peace and Love in my life comes through Loving myself fully.

When I Love myself fully, I Love my mistakes and my habits and my dreams. I can only Change things I Love about myself. I can only Change myself. When I Love myself fully, I Allow and Accept other people as they are because all the Love in my life I get from myself. When I look to others to provide Love in my life, I feel incomplete. When I Love myself fully, I remember that all the Love in my life is within me Now Here.

To Love myself fully is a habit I have to develop and foster. It takes one month of making a consistent Choice all day every day to form a new habit. Sometimes new habits form in a time frame that is quicker than one month when they closely match habits I already have in place. Sometimes a new habit can take longer than one month when I AM replacing an old deeply ingrained habit with a new one.

My current experiences in my life are a result of my current habits in my thoughts, feelings, words, and actions. If I wonder what my current habits are, I have only to look at my current life experiences that result from my consistent Choices. If I keep doing the same things, I shall keep getting the same results.

In my past, I Choose the garbage in(side of me) garbage out(side of me) habit system. This system allowed the garbage in(side of me) to manifest as the garbage out(side of me).

Now I Choose the God In(side of me) God Out(side of me) habit system. I Choose this by Asking for, Aligning with, Allowing, and Accepting God's Greatness In(side of me).

Being disconnected or Connected to God is a Choice
I Claim my Connection with God through my voice

I let go of desperately needing to pursue and manifest anything in my experience. I Align with, Allow, and Accept God within me as my Source and Supply. When I Align with God, I Align with God's Vision for my life. God's Vision of my life in this very moment is the Most Loving, Peaceful, Joyous, Abundant, Successful, and Miraculous idea I can Imagine.

Since God is All of Life. I AM Connected with God. The only way I can be disconnected from God is through a Choice to be disconnected. I Choose either to be disconnected or Connected. It is a Choice only I can make about my life.

When I feel disconnected, I immediately use my Creative Powers within my thoughts, feelings, words, and actions to Claim with my entire Heart, Mind, and Being that I AM One with God Right Here Right Now. This habit powerfully Connects me again. It is a simple Choice.

I Breathe in Deeply and use God's name (AH) I exhale deeply (OM) and transform my tension back into the energy of God

The simple Choice of Connecting with God sometimes is caught up in my emotionally guided opinions. When this is my experience, I thank my ego and bless my ego and release my ego. I thank and bless my ego because I can only release the things I Love and Accept about myself. I Choose this until it forms a new habit for me.

When I need to release more tension from my being, I take the time to meditate. I breathe in deeply, I pronounce the name of God (AH), and I visualise that I breathe in the Love of God deeply. I exhale deeply, and I pronounce the name of God's Gratitude (OM) to transform my released tension back into God's Loving, Successful, and Abundant Energy. All of the Energy of the Universe is Loving, Successful, and Abundant, but my perceptions of it may be something different.

I Choose habits that foster and support my Connection to God and my Connection to the Loving, Peaceful, Joyous, Abundant, Successful, and Miraculous Nature of God. It is my Choice.

I AM SPIRITUAL HAPPINESS

I let go of desperately needing to pursue and manifest anything in my experience.

God's Vision of my life in this very moment is the most Loving, Peaceful, Joyous, Abundant, Successful, and Miraculous idea I can Imagine.

I AM Time Happiness

Life is Timeless when I AM One with God
Life is Present when I AM One with God
When Life flows Easily
Life flows Happily
What time is it?
Time for a new adventure is it?
God is the Only Power
Now is the Only Place of Power
Cycles of Life take their Time
Sow, Nurture, and Reap
All from my Mind

I AM Time Happiness

Life is Timeless when I AM One with God
Life is Present when I AM One with God

All of Life is an illusion. God, Love, and Life supports the framework of Free Will. Free Will supports the manifestation of any belief I Choose. As a result, Life supports the belief in Unity of All That Is; We Are One. Life also supports the belief in separation from All That Is; there appears to be separate people, places, and things in the experience of Life when I Choose to believe that.

There is Only Oneness. God experiencing God.

God is like a bicycle wheel. The spokes on the wheel represent the different paths I can take to Connect with God. I AM always Connected with God, however in my beliefs I can imagine being separate from the central Hub of God. As I journey in my life, there are times when I feel a deep and real Connection with God and there are times when I feel a definite disconnection from God. Both are only Chosen perceptions within me.

In my journey to Accept my Oneness with God I have travelled on many spokes. On some I felt evil and worthless, while on others I felt totally worthy and alive. I spent my time jumping from spoke to spoke searching for my fullest Connection with God. On each new spoke, I gained a whole new set of knowledge and beliefs, instead of accepting that my Oneness with God Just Is.

My Connection to God was, is, and shall always Be Oneness. Even so, my perception of my connection with God can be whatever I Choose.

My feelings about time, mirror my feelings about God. When time seems slow, it mirrors my disconnection with All That Is. I imagine I am separate from the things I desire to experience.

When life becomes timeless and I AM in the Flow of life, I AM One with God. When I AM in the Now, I AM Present with All That Is and I AM One with God.

When the bicycle wheel image is expanded into three

dimensions, it is a good image of God and Time for me. God is the Point of Light at the Centre of All That Is. Each spoke that radiates from the centre appears to have different characteristics. Each spoke appears to be separate from every other spoke. Yet All spokes have the same Source.

All spokes have the same Source and occur at the same Time. In this 3-D version of God and Time, there is Only NOW. One spoke represents the Big Bang. One Spoke represents My Life. One Spoke represents the Big Crunch as the end of our current universal experience has been described. We Are One, All That Is, Only Now.

The Past and Future are Only places I can visit in my imagination. There are no trips to the Past and Future. There is Only Now.

When Life flows Easily
Life flows Happily

When I fully envelope myself in and enjoy whatever is Right Here Right Now, Life flows easily and Life flows Happily.

Unhappiness results in denying and fighting the experiences that are Right Here Right Now. Unhappiness is experienced when I try to control and change other people, places, and things in my experience. Unhappiness is a result of my unmet expectations. Unhappiness is only chosen inside of me. Hell is my inability to control and change and love whatever is Now Here.

Heaven is my ability to Allow and Accept and Love whatever is Now Here. When I go with the flow, I experience Heaven in my life. Happiness is a natural consequence of releasing the things that make me unhappy in life. Whatever I focus on, I energize, and I attract into my life. Unhappy thoughts energize and attract unhappy experiences. Happy thoughts energize and attract Happy experiences. My Happy thoughts can Only be focussed upon, energized, and attracted within me, by me.

When I Live fully in the Now Moment, Life flows easily and Happily. No matter what I do in life (artist, writer, father, banker, plumber, doctor, unemployed), my ability to share my Happiness with others is a Now Moment experience.

What time is it?
Time for a new adventure is it?

God provides me with my life and all the time that makes up my life. God allows me to view time in anyway I Choose. I can imagine that I have little time to accomplish the dreams I envision. I can also Choose to Know that everything I could ever dream about at the deepest heartfelt most secret levels comes to me always in all ways in the right ways and at the right time.

When I live with a feeling of God's Time freedom, my life is an experience of Lasting Freedom. God always provides me with enough time, energy, and resources to be, do, and have the things that God would have me be, do, and have in my life. There are no unrealistic dreams in the Mind of God, there are only unrealistic time lines in the minds of human beings.

What time is it? Right Now it is the time for me to be, do, and have whatever brings me the most Happiness as well as serving God in others.

Time for a new adventure is it? When time seems slow and every experience is boring, it is time for a new adventure in my life. It is time for me to let go of my expectations and to Let God Be my experiences.

God is the only Power
Now is the Only Place of Power

When I am distracted by my thoughts of other people, places, and things outside of me, I step outside of God's Power within me.

God is the Point of Power Central to All Life. The Now is the Only Place to access God's Power. The Only way to access

God in the Now is by being in the flow within me. When my thoughts are One with God, then I AM One with the Power of God.

Cycles of Life take their Time
Sow, Nurture, and Reap
All from my Mind

In the moment I AM One with God, wherein I experience Oneness without any separation, my experience manifests instantaneously. Until that moment, I experience the cycles of time. Every thought I sow, nurture, and reap in my mind comes to pass. To know what I sow, nurture, and reap in my mind, I have only to look at my experiences. I Chose everything.

I AM TIME HAPPINESS

In the moment I AM One with God,
wherein I experience Oneness without any
separation, my experience manifests instantaneously.

I AM Abundance Happiness

God is Love, Success, and Abundance
Even Abundant lack is still Abundance
Money is Only One form of Abundance
Air, Water, and Laughter are also Abundance
Anything that can I exchange with others is Abundance
I Give my Abundance and I Live God's Abundance
In every moment, it is my Choice to feel and Be Abundance
What I feel deeply is my blueprint for Abundance
Happiness always comes before Abundance
For the process to Be Lasting
Happiness leads to Abundance

I AM Abundance Happiness

I AM ABUNDANCE HAPPINESS

If Life were the opposite of Abundance, Life would cease to exist. Everything in life would proceed in a downward spiral of destruction and decay until All That Is no longer existed.

However that is not the case. Life is Abundance. Everything in Life proceeds in a cycle of birth and death and birth again. Although some forms may no longer be present in the process, the Spirit of Life is forever Abundant and supports All That Is in various forms.

God is Love, Success, and Abundance
Even Abundant lack is still Abundance

God is All That Is. God pours God's Spirit into all that is. God is Love, Success, and Abundance. God also supports fear, failure, and lack in the physical experience in order that God's Love, Success, and Abundance may Be perceived. Both Abundance and the opposite, Abundant lack, use the principle of Abundance to Manifest.

In the experience of Oneness with God, everything is Right Here Right Now. All Times, Places, Knowledge, and Experiences are Right Here Right Now. There is no separation. Instead of being on an outside spoke of God's 3-D bicycle wheel, I AM the Central Hub and Oneness is Whole and Complete within my Core.

A mere thought from me Attracts another part of my experience. The concept of Abundance and lack are One and the same. They are both Abundance. My thoughts draw from the Pure Potential of God/Life/Energy my experiences of Abundance.

On Earth, the experience of time and space provides the framework necessary for the gradual experience of Abundance and the seemingly varying degrees of Abundance. These are only my perception. There is Only Abundance.

Money is Only One form of Abundance
Air, Water, and Laughter are also Abundance

Money has become the most accepted means of exchange in the human experience. Money has an immense amount of power associated with it. This power becomes exaggerated by the feelings people attached to money. Money is Only One form of Abundance.

Absolutely everything in Life is a result of Abundance. Everything I experience is a form of Abundance. Air, Water, Flowers, Knowledge, Paper, Poverty, War, Grass, and Laughter are all forms of Abundance.

Anything that can I exchange with others is Abundance
I Give my Abundance and I Live God's Abundance

Anything I can use in a form of trade is a form of Abundance. Water, Flowers, Knowledge, Paper, Poverty, War, Grass, and Laughter can all be traded for other forms of Abundance, be it money, house, wisdom, or anything else.

Part of the confusion around Abundance is the external focus on the particular form of Abundance known as money. Life is a manifestation of thoughts, feelings, words, and actions. When my thoughts, feelings, words, and actions are focussed on money only, they can just as easily repel the form of money as they can attract it into my life.

My entire being is like a piece of paper upon which I write my desires to the Universe. I use my thoughts, feelings, words, and actions to place my request with God. God cares not what I ask for. God Unconditionally Loves me and gives me whatever I ask for. God is like an immense photocopier that takes my written request, which I create through my energy use and then reproduces it until I change my written request.

In every moment, it is my Choice to feel and Be Abundance
What I feel deeply is my blueprint for Abundance

What I Give, I Live. Everything I believe is embodied within my energy aura and is reproduced and sent back to me with no questions asked. In my past, there have been many times I believed I placed an order for a large amount of Abundance when I may have actually placed an order for a large amount of lack.

The most powerful currency in my life is my Attention. Wherever I place my attention, I place my intention. In my experience, when I place my attention on 1% fear, doubt, or worry, I actually intend fear, doubt, or worry 100% in that very moment. That also goes to say that when I place my attention on 1% Love, Faith, Certainty, I intend Love, Faith, Certainty 100% in that very moment.

In my past, I have changed my order with the Universe constantly. One moment, I Chose to be Connected and Believe I AM Abundance (one page to be photocopied), and then in the next moment, I chose to feel disconnected from Abundance (another page to be photocopied).

When things have gone bad in my life they are a result of my Choices. I have Chosen one belief and stuck with it until I experienced the manifestation of the that belief.

When things have gone well in my life they are a result of my Choices. I have Chosen one belief and stuck with it until I experienced the manifestation of that belief.

Whatever belief, I think, feel, say, or act upon becomes my blueprint for Abundance. Abundance takes the forms of Absolutely everything present in my Life. The words God, Love, Life, Abundance, Change, and Success are all interchangeable. Whatever I experience is a manifestation of Abundance in my Life.

Happiness always comes before Abundance
For the process to Be Lasting
Happiness leads to Abundance

My Intentions are made up of my beliefs in Abundance. When I feel that I am lacking, I make Choices that support lack in my experience, my unhappy and insecure feelings lead to Abundant lack.

When I Feel Abundant, Life Flows and Happiness and Abundance abounds. My Feelings of inner Happiness and Security Manifest Abundance easily.

Happiness is a Choice I make to Feel Connected with All That Is. Abundance is a Result of Feeling Connected with All That Is. Heaven is my Ability to Align with, Allow, Accept, and Love All the Abundance Now Here, no matter what appears to be.

I AM ABUNDANCE HAPPINESS

When I Feel Abundant, Life Flows and Happiness and Abundance abounds.

My Feelings of inner Happiness and Security Manifest Abundance easily.

I AM Relationship Happiness

We Are All One
Separation is an Illusion
Relationships help me Feel Whole
Perception of Unity is my goal
The greatest challenges I have are within me
Although I imagine they come from society
My inability to control and change
Is One with my ability to Allow and Accept
I can Only Choose One Intention Now
Whatever I Choose becomes
my Relationships Now

I AM Relationship Happiness

I AM RELATIONSHIP HAPPINESS

My life is an experience of relationships with all people, places, and things. If something is in my experience I have a relationship with it. This includes the people, places, and things that challenge me. Absolutely everything I experience in my life is manifested by God through the energy pathways of my thoughts, feelings, words, and actions.

We Are All One
Separation is an Illusion

God Is All. Everything is a Manifestation of God. God is Absolutely Everything in experience. When I perceive life from the largest perspective, I recognize the interconnectedness of All That Is. I think, feel, speak, and act from and for the highest perspective. We Are All One.

Separation is an Illusion. The Illusion of separation is something only I can Choose using my thoughts, feelings, words, and actions. When I Choose the Illusion of separation, I Choose to feel disconnected from All That Is, I experience what I call and believe is disconnection and separation, yet everything is actually One. When I Choose to deny my connection to All That Is, I experience disconnection by my beliefs.

We Are All One. We are all from the same Source. We are constantly in touch with the Source and Power that is God. At the simplest form, We Are All One can be expressed as *I AM.*

I AM Whole and Complete. I AM Abundance. God Is All. I AM One with God. God is All within me. I AM God.

Relationships help me Feel Whole
Perception of Unity is my goal

Perception of Unity with all of life is my goal. I AM One

with All That Is. Perception is a thinking process. My Connection with All That Is expresses itself fully through my Joy and Potential. When I feel Joyously Connected to my Potential, I AM One with God. Joy is my Compass. Any thought and feeling that Uplifts and Encourages my Joy and Potential promotes my Connection with All That Is.

In my relationships with all the people in my life, I feel what I sense as obvious disconnection or Connection. Even without knowing a particular person sometimes I sense feelings that express opposition or Alignment to a particular person upon first meeting.

Feelings as immediate sensations within my body, without any story attached to them, can be very helpful. These feelings for me are the voice of God Giving Ongoing Direction. With God Giving Ongoing Direction, I feel an overall sense of well being.

When the feelings within my body are more extreme through the story that I win with this particular experience or lose without it, then I AM very often being influenced by my emotionally guided opinions (ego) believing I must fight to win.

The greatest challenges J have are within me
Although J imagine they come from society

The greatest challenges I experience in my life, I imagine come through my relationships with society outside of me. In my past, I have fought, denied, and struggled against my outer experience when it did not suit me.

Whatever I Align with, Allow, and Accept within my being becomes Attracted and Manifested as my experience. Whatever I AM presently experiencing, I have Aligned with, Allowed, and Accepted within my being as my reality. That is the reason that my imagination is as powerful as my perceived reality. Whatever belief I AM One with I Create.

All my relationship challenges with people in my life are actually an out-picturing of my beliefs about the people in my experience. Whatever I believe, I receive. If I believe that the people in my life are loving and compassionate with All Life, that is what I experience.

To know what I believe, I only have to look at what I currently receive. If I would like to experience different forms in my relationships, I have but to Align with, Allow, and Accept different beliefs about my life. Life is a journey to Accepting that Oneness with All That Is. Whether I start that process Now or never is a decision only I can make for myself. Everyone else in my experience makes the same decision for themselves as well

My inability to control and change
Is One with my ability to Allow and Accept

The greatest challenge to my Relationship Happiness is also my Greatest Blessing. I get to Choose what I experience in All my Relationships. No one else can Choose what I experience. I Choose it. In my past, I have Chosen Heaven and I have Chosen hell at different times.

Hell is my inability to control and change and love whatever is Now Here. My need to control and change things is a result of my belief that whatever is Now Here takes me away from what I desire to be in life.

No matter what I believe about my life, I always accomplish my purpose for my life with God. Heaven is my ability to Allow and Accept and Love whatever is Now Here. Whatever is Now Here is God's Present Presents Presence.

My inability to control and change is One with my ability to Allow and Accept because they are both Choices I can make to Create and View and Attract my life as I Choose.

I can Only Choose One Intention Now
Whatever I Choose becomes
my Relationships Now

God Manifests through my life whatever I Intend with my entire Being. I Choose everything in my life. I Choose my Relationship Connections to All That Is in Life; Love, Success, Abundance, Livelihood, and Absolutely everything else I experience.

I AM RELATIONSHIP HAPPINESS

*God Manifests through my life whatever
I Intend with my entire Being.*

I AM Freedom Happiness

Life is Happiness
Freedom is Happiness
I make all of my Life Choices
Freedom and Happiness are Choices
I can Imagine my life is Limitless and Free
Or I can Imagine my life is limited by society
God/ Heart Thanks and Loves It
ego/ mind thinks in limits
Both Heaven and hell
Are my Choices
As well

I AM Freedom Happiness

I AM FREEDOM HAPPINESS

Life is Happiness
Freedom is Happiness

In my past, I have easily imagined that Happiness was a result of what I experienced rather than a result of what I believed. Happiness is the Cause of Happiness in my life.

Whatever I believe at the deepest part of my being becomes what I experience. God's Energy Manifests my life through whatever I believe. When I believe Love, Success, Abundance, and Happiness are in my life, I experience Love, Success, Abundance, and Happiness. This fact holds true with every belief I Choose.

I make all of my Life Choices
Freedom and Happiness are Choices

When I take full Responsibility for my life, I Accept that I make all my Choices. I Choose everything in my life. My beliefs imbue all my actions and Attract all my experiences. My Intentions form my life.

At the highest Vibrational Energy Rate my Intention for life mirrors God's Intention for my life. When my Intention is One with God's for my life, Freedom and Happiness abound in my life. Freedom and Happiness abound because Absolutely every experience in my life leads to the Manifestation of my dreams and Oneness with God.

Before I embodied into my present life experience, I planned (with God) the purpose of my life as well as the challenges to oppose me reaching the fulfilment of my purpose. Both my purpose and my challenges come through my thoughts and feelings about my life. The Attainment of my Purpose with God is assured in life, just as much as the realty that I Choose it.

On Earth there are almost seven billion purposes being

accomplished Right Here Right Now. God works them all together with absolute perfection. The precision of such an experience is amazing considering that each of the almost seven billion people have the Freedom to make any choice at any time. There are no unrealistic dreams in the Mind of God. There are only unrealistic time lines in the mind of humans. Every thing happens in the right way and at the right time for all concerned on Earth.

I can Imagine my life is Limitless and Free Or I can Imagine my life is limited by society

Happiness is a Choice. All of life is a Choice. My Choice for Happiness is the Cause of my Happiness. Whatever I Choose I experience. Whatever I Choose is what I Live. What I Live, I Give. What I Give, I Live.

All of my life Manifests from what I Give myself in my thoughts, feelings, words, and actions. I can Choose to Imagine my life in any way. I can Imagine my life as being Limitless and Free or limited by the beliefs of society. I Choose it All.

God/Heart Thanks and Loves It ego/mind thinks in limits

My ego (emotionally guided opinions) uses my mind to think in limits. My ego mind thinks within certain limits and believes in limited possibilities. In my past, my ego mind spoke in what seemed like limitless possibilities. However limitless possibilities in my limited ego mind equals limitations. Ego mind thinks in stories and uses emotions to convince me that I win with a particular experience or lose without it.

My Heart is the home of God within me. My God Heart Thanks and Loves It (It being whatever I AM Now Here). My God Heart use Feelings and Impressions to show me that I can be, do, or have any experience. My God Heart does not worry about what experience I have, or connections I have, or abilities I have in place.

God Gives Ongoing Direction through the still small voice that suggests things to me without any real urgency attached to these suggestions. God has spoken to me in a very clear voice and with a definite sense of urgency when my physical life was in immediate danger. I Thank God for this very obvious and clear communication.

Most of the communication God presents feels good and is without any desire to influence me one way or the other. I may enjoy the new direction or Choose a different one. God is Happy in all ways. I Choose to be Happy first through my thoughts and feelings.

Both Heaven and hell
Are my Choices
As well

I Choose absolutely everything in my life. I Choose all of my thoughts and feelings. I Choose the life I desire to lead and the paths I follow. I Choose my dreams and their manifestation. I Choose the relationships I wish to foster and develop. I Choose all the experiences and challenges that I have. Challenges in my life remind me that only I can Choose to Align with, Allow, and Accept God as the Source and Supply of my life. I Choose it All.

I Choose whether I AM Happiness first and foremost in my experience or not. When I Choose to be Happiness no matter what I experience, I experience Happiness no matter what I experience. It is a Choice Only I can make.

There is only experience. Heaven or hell is Only my perception of my experience. Some people may call an experience hell, while others may call it Heaven because of their perceptions about that experience.

For me hell is my inability to change or control or love whatever is Now Here, while Heaven is my ability to Allow and

Accept and Love whatever is Now Here Happily. I AM Free to Choose whatever I decide.

I AM FREEDOM HAPPINESS

God Gives Ongoing Direction through the still small voice that suggests things to me without any real urgency attached to these suggestions.

God has spoken to me in a very clear voice and with a definite sense of urgency when my physical life was in immediate danger.

I Thank God for this very obvious and clear communication. Most of the communication God presents feels good and is without any desire to influence me one way or the other.

I may enjoy the new direction or Choose a different one. God is Happy in all ways. I Choose to be Happy first through my thoughts and feelings.

I AM Lasting Happiness

Less attitude
More Gratitude
Think less, Thank More
Attach less, Detach More
All of Life Supports my Feelings
I can doubt God's Support or Feel It
Happiness is not a travel destination in life
Happiness is the way to travel through my life
Pessimists find challenges and love to blame
Optimists find solutions for the same
Happy people Love Life's game

I AM Lasting Happiness

I AM LASTING HAPPINESS

Success is getting what I love in life. Happiness is loving what I get in life. Lasting Happiness is a Choice I make to Enjoy All That Is. Lasting Happiness is simple when things progress with ease. Lasting Happiness comes when I Align with, Allow, and Accept the Presence of God in my Life. The words Happiness, Gratitude, and God are interchangeable. So are the words unhappiness, attitude, and ego.

Less attitude
More Gratitude

Gratitude is Humble and Happy, while attitude is demanding and aggressive. My Gratitude or attitude becomes the ground where I sow my dreams. My Gratitude or attitude becomes the nourishment I use to nurture my dreams. My Gratitude or attitude become the way I harvest my dreams.

When I have attitude, my ego is active. When I Choose attitude in my life, I Choose the farmer of my life to be my ego. Everything I sow, I also reap. Whatever I Give, I Live. When I Give attitude, I Live attitude. When I doubt God's Support, All of Life Supports my feelings of doubt.

God is active in my life when I Choose Gratitude. When I Choose Gratitude in my life, I experience Lasting Happiness as I experience Oneness with All That Is. When I feel God's Support, All of Life Supports my feelings of God.

Think less, Thank More
Attach less, Detach More

Detachment and Happiness and Love are the best of friends. As soon as I become attached to something I leave myself open to the possible experience of unhappiness and fear.

When I think, I become attached to my ideas of what I need to experience in life. My ego mind thinks its way into so many ideas and miseries. My ego mind becomes attached to limited ideas of Happiness.

God Heart Detaches from particular people, places, things, and experiences and Loves All That Is. Lasting Happiness results through Detachment. Detachment supports Happiness and Love because All That Is Now Here is absolutely perfect. God Planned it. God Manifested it. God Is All. I may Choose whatever I Choose.

All of Life Supports my Feelings
I can doubt God's Support or Feel It

The more I AM Grateful and Detached, the more I experience Happiness. All of Life supports my Feelings. God, Love, and Life have no interest in what I Choose to Feel. God, Love, and Life only Manifest my energy use before me.

I can doubt God's Support or Feel God's Support. I can only Choose One or the other in each moment. To Feel Happiness is both cause and consequence. I Choose Happiness and I experience Happiness.

Happiness is not a travel destination in life
Happiness is the way to travel through my life

Happiness is a feeling, not a form. Some forms seem to mirror my Happiness, yet they are not the cause of my Happiness. God is the Cause of All That Is, including my Happiness. God is the Energy within All Life. Heaven, God, and Nirvana are not some place I arrive at in the future. They are the Gratitude that support my Joy and Lasting Happiness Right Now.

Pessimists find challenges and love to blame
Optimists find solutions for the same
Happy people Love Life's game

Happy People exude an Energy of Lasting Happiness. Others Feel it and Love it and Share it. Life is a Game of Lasting Happiness to Enjoy.

I AM LASTING HAPPINESS

Happy People exude an
Energy of Lasting Happiness.
Others Feel it and Love it and Share it.
Life is a Game of Lasting Happiness to Enjoy.

Hell is my inability to
control and change and love
whatever is Now Here

Heaven is my ability to
Allow and Accept and Love
whatever is Now Here

ONE MONTH TO LASTING HAPPINESS

I design Affirmations to help me through tough times, When my life shows me that my Intentions and Attention do not match where I desire to go in life. I Choose to foster thoughts and feelings that Connect to my Joy and Potential. I wrote these Affirmations to Activate and Attract my Lasting Happiness. I call this section One Month to Lasting Happiness because habits take time to form. Each day I Activate Affirmations with Feeling to help me to redefine, guide, and inspire my eternal internal Connection to the Creative Power Within me.

God Gives Ongoing Direction to my Joy and Potential Always in All Ways.

God Loves Me

God is All of Life. Absolutely every person, place, thing, and experience in my life is God. God Supports and Loves all my choices through Free Will. I can Choose Heaven or hell and like a photocopier, God reproduces whatever I Choose. Hell is my inability to control or change or love whatever is Now Here. Heaven is my ability to Allow and Accept and Love whatever is Now Here. I Intend to Choose things that make me feel Loved, Abundant, Successful, Happy, Cared for, and Miraculous in every moment and especially when things are rough.

I Love Myself Fully

I love others and God fully; All of Life; every person, place, thing, and experience. I love my mistakes and my habits and my dreams. I can only Change things I love about myself. I Can only Change myself. When I love myself fully, I allow people to be who they are because my love comes from a feeling inside of me. When I love myself fully, I respect that other people may wish to do something different. I respect the space of others and they respect my space. When I Choose to enter other people's spaces in ways that make them feel uncomfortable, other people enter my space in ways that make me feel uncomfortable. The need to criticize or make fun of others or to be part of the crowd is a need to feel love inside myself. When I love myself fully, I love others fully as they are showing up and it is easy for me to love and bless them. When I Love myself fully, my love Attracts my experiences.

One Month to New Habits

It takes one month of making a Choice (consistently all day every day) to form a new habit. Once a habit is in place, it <u>can take more</u>

<u>than</u> one month to reprogram it by making a different choice (consistently all day every day). My current experiences in life come from my current habits. If I keep my current habits, I keep creating the same experiences. I admit and accept that many of my past experiences have been painful with my Chosen habits. Before I used the garbage in, garbage out habit system. The garbage in(side of me) became the garbage out(side of me). Right Now I let go and I let God. To let go of my old habits it takes at least one month of consistent work Choosing a new habit. To let God, I Choose new habits so that I Align with, Allow, and Accept God's time schedule for the manifestation of my dreams. When I Align with, Allow, and Accept where I desire to be over where I believe I am, then I experience my dreams in physical form.

Thank you ego for my emotionally guided opinions

I bless you and thank you and release you as I accept God Giving Ongoing Direction in this very moment which suggests I can Choose beliefs and habits that promote and support the most Loving, Successful, Abundant, Peaceful, and Miraculous experience Right Here Right Now. Mistakes are only habits that take me away from where I desire to be. I make mistakes as I create new habits until I have fully accepted my new habits. I get out of my ego mind and release all my emotionally guided opinions about what is Now Here in relation to what came before. Without opinions and only my intention for enjoyment, I Align with, Allow, and Accept the enjoyment of God/Life/Energy Right Now. My ego mind thinks in limits. My God Heart Thanks and Loves It.

I AM Healthy

I make healthy habits through my choices. For my body, I Choose to eat healthy and nourishing food, exercise regularly, brush and floss my teeth after every meal, and get plenty of rest. For my mind, I Choose to love all my thoughts, feelings, words, actions, and I Choose to love every person, place, thing, and experience in my life as best I can. I can find at least one thing I love about everything in my life. For my spirit, I Choose to Connect with God as much as possible each and every moment of my life.

God Is My Power

God is the Power within everything. God does everything without me. God does everything without the most powerful people in the world. When a powerful person dies, the world is still here. Everything in my life is attracted to me by what I believe about myself at the very deepest part of my being. I Intend to Align with, Allow, and Accept God as the Power of my life. I become Powerful when I become Power Smart. Power Smart people clean up their garbage in(side) and clean up their garbage out(side). I Choose to clean up my feelings of love and worthiness with God in(side of me). I Choose to keep myself clean, my clothes clean, my room clean, and my house clean out(side of me). I AM Power Smart with all the energy I use. I only use the Power I require, so that as much of God's Power expressed through me as possible is available and focused on my dreams.

I AM Calm and Peaceful

I Choose to slow down and take all the time I need to see and feel God in every person, place, thing, and experience. I Intend to be calm, respectful, loving, honest, and trustworthy with myself and everyone.

I AM Happy

I Intend to use appropriate humor and I make sure everyone is having fun and is comfortable. The way I know everyone is enjoying themselves occurs when I take the time to recognize that everyone is laughing genuinely. The only way I can tell that someone is genuinely happy is to notice how other people are acting and reacting with me. When everyone is Happy, the experience is a Win-Win for everyone.

I AM Responsible

I AM the only one responsible for my life. I AM Only Responsible for me. I AM the only one who can Choose my habits. I AM the only one who can Change my habits. I Choose everything I feel. I Choose to release my disappointments, anger, and frustrations without hurting myself or others. I Choose to be Happy over being right. I Choose to help myself and others be happy in respectful ways. Responsibility is my ability to respond appropriately with All of Life.

I Intend God

God provides everything in life. I rarely get the things I desire when I pursue them. I always get the things I desire when I Attract them. The only way to Attract something into my life is by changing my inner world. I Intend to Change my world experience from garbage in(side) garbage out(side) to Greatness In(side) Greatness Out(side). I foster and create this change by consciously studying my new chosen beliefs and habits until they become my unconscious beliefs and habits. I Intend to deeply Love, Trust, Respect, and be Honest with myself and God (Absolutely everything in life). I Intend this 100%. 100% is like being pregnant. There is no 50% pregnant. A woman is either pregnant (100%) or not (0%). Life provides whatever I Intend. Either I Intend (100%) or I do not (0%). Wherever I place my Attention, I place my Intention in my experience. When I place my Attention on my 1% fear, doubt, or worry, I Intend fear, doubt, or worry 100% in that moment. Similarly, when I place my Attention on my 1% Love, Faith, Certainty, I Intend Love, Faith, Certainty 100% in that moment. In life, I Intend God 100% or I Intend anything other than God. When challenging experiences enter my life, I AM out of Alignment with God and my purpose in life. When amazing things happen, I AM in Alignment with God and my purpose in life.

J Thank God

When things are challenging I take the time to consciously connect with God. I breathe in deeply, and I breathe in the Love of God deeply. I exhale deeply, and I pronounce the name of God (AH) to transform my released tension back into God's Energy. I take the time to meditate in this fashion as often during the day as I require to feel totally Connected with God in my life. I can Choose to feel disconnected or I Choose to Feel Connected. It is a Choice only I can make. The Choices I can make Connect me with totally different results. I Intend to Choose New Habits of Feeling Connected with God Always in All Ways. Thank You God for our Powerful Connection and for Your Power Providing everything in my Life. With God, I have the most Loving, Successful, Abundant, Peaceful, and Miraculous Habits Right Here Right Now.

Joy Is My Compass

Absolutely every thought and feeling I use in a day (and there are thousands and thousands I use in a given day), combine to form my Core Intention, unless and until I specify my Core Intention in the moment **Right Now**. The great confusion of being the Creator of my own Experience is that in my past, I unconsciously Choose my habitual thoughts and feelings as my Core Intention. When the Creations that resulted in my life were far from my desires I could not understand the way in which I had Chosen what was in my experience. **Right Now** using Joy as my Compass, I can Consciously Choose my Core Intention. My Core Intention Creates a Vibration which Attracts my Experiences. The process of Creating my Own Experience Consciously and Constantly Accesses, Activates, and Attracts Joy in three specific ways:

Intend Joy
Feel Joy
Choose Joy

These Affirmations bless my life powerfully.

ONE MONTH TO LASTING HAPPINESS

When I place my Attention on my 1% fear, doubt, or worry, I Intend fear, doubt, or worry 100% in that moment.

Similarly, when I place my Attention on my 1% Love, Faith, Certainty, I Intend Love, Faith, Certainty 100% in that moment.

Affirmations of my Happiness

Right Now is the Only moment of Creation and the Only Access point to All That Is.

God/Life/Energy is Pure Potential awaiting my focus and attention.

I Ask for, Align with, Allow, and Accept God/Life/Energy to Manifest in my life when I AM One with All That Is.

The following pages are Affirmations of my Happiness. They are words I have used to Ask for, Align with, Allow, and Accept that my Happiness is Right Here Right Now. Only I can Align with my Manifestations. God/Life/Energy can Only Manifest in physicality where I AM in Conscious reality.

I AM Happy and Peacefully Blessed in my life
and I Open to my fullest Potential of Love,
Success, and Abundance by Joyfully Blessing
the potential, the good, and the possible
in the lives of All That Is.

I Ask for, Align with, Allow, and Accept this
Object of my Desires and God sees that we are One.

I Create my Artistic Creations because it brings me
Joy to Share them. God handles the details that
Allow me to Share them with others in the
Right way and Right time.

No matter what appears to be, the world is a
Loving, Successful and Abundant place waiting for
me to Claim all the Love, Success, and
Abundance I Choose.

I Allow what is to be what is, while I focus on my
path of God's Pure Potential in my life.

God's Goodness is my ability to express
Freely when I Choose.

I Choose thoughts, feelings, words, and actions that
support my experience of God's Love, Success,
Abundance, Peace, Health, and Joy.

Happiness and Joy are Felt when I AM Love
Absolutely, Unconditionally, Totally,
and Fantastically.

All the Joy and Happiness I shall ever experience
within my life is available within me Right Now.

No person, place, thing, or experience makes me
Happy or takes my Happiness from me
unless and until I Choose.

I AM Humble, Generous, and Grateful with
others and myself and God provides
for me in the same spirit.

I take time to Feel Love, Success, Abundance,
Peace, Health, and Joy within me, so that
God provides them without me.

I let go of my expectations and
Let God provide my perfections.

When I AM Now Here
God is Now Here with me.

Every person, place, thing, and experience I encounter helps to Manifest my dreams as I have Imagined them in my deepest heartfelt most secret beliefs, no matter what appears to be.

My mind can only hold one thought at a time. My mind can hold one thought of my fear and limitations, or my mind can hold one thought of my Good and my God. My thoughts are my responsibility to Choose.

What would bring me the most Joy Right Here Right Now and serve others in the process?

What is the Happiest thought I can Imagine in the situation Right Here Right Now?

Life is set up for me to win.
When I AM feeling good, I am letting my
Happiest Dreams in.

I
always
win when I
let go of trying to
change, Create, get, or
improve the particular people,
places, and things in my outer experience,
and instead I let The Feeling of God
within me attract the perfect people,
places, and things for
me to experience my
own energy use
in physical
forms.

ABOUT THE AUTHOR

Barry Thomas Bechta is an artist, author, and film maker whose work centers around the concepts of Unconditional Love. Barry knew he wanted to write from a very young age and was encouraged with his artistic skills and only began writing full time in his thirties. He wrote his first book, *I AM Creating My Own Experience* as a personal journal to choose connection with God/Life/Energy. He has since written 17 inspirational spiritual books.

Barry loves to hear from people whom have connected with his writing and used it as a tool to improve their lives. If you would like to write him about your personal experiences as a result of reading any of his books, Barry encourages you to do so.

You can also get a Free Digital Copy of *I AM Creating My Own Experience - The Creation Vibration* from his main website:

www.unconditionallovebooks.com

Barry Thomas Bechta is available for interviews, special events, workshops, and lectures that redefine, guide, and inspire everyone's connection to the Creative Power within themselves. To arrange author interviews, special events, workshops, or lectures, please contact:

UNCONDITIONAL
LOVE BOOKS

Unconditional Love Books
Box # 610 - 2527 Pine St.,
Vancouver, BC, Canada V6J 3E8

info@unconditionallovebooks.com

www.unconditionallovebooks.com

For additional copies of Barry's books, products, and services please contact your local book seller. Many products and services are Only available to order directly from the publisher as eProducts on the website.

Thanks for your purchase and Remember to Consciously Create your Life.

Right Now is the Only Moment of Creation

Enjoy it Fully!

www.ingramcontent.com/pod-product-compliance
Lightning Source LLC
Chambersburg PA
CBHW031522040426
42445CB00009B/358